FINANCE
MATTER$!

Leann Voss, IYR, LLC

FINANCE
MATTER$!

EXPLORING YOUR ASSETS AND
SECURING YOUR FUTURE

Tate Publishing & Enterprises

Published by Tate Publishing & Enterprises, LLC
127 E. Trade Center Terrace | Mustang, Oklahoma 73064 USA
1.888.361.9473 | www.tatepublishing.com

Tate Publishing is committed to excellence in the publishing industry. The company reflects the philosophy established by the founders, based on Psalm 68:11,
"The Lord gave the word and great was the company of those who published it."

Published in the United States of America

ISBN: 978-1-61663-326-4
1. Juvenile Nonfiction / Concepts / Money
10.05.21

Dedication

For Walt, to whom I say, "Ditto."

Acknowledgments

I convey my heartfelt appreciation to three authors I have never met. Each man wrote his personal philosophy in book form so I could read and decide how I felt about it. To Richard J. Foster, M. Scott Peck, and Richard J. Mayberry I say, "Thank you for sharing your heart with me. Thank you for helping me on my journey."

I thank Troy Capps, my dad, who looked me in the eye and gave me this challenge: "Know what you believe and why you believe it."

I give a profound thank you to my mother, Jan Capps, who brought me home and loves me to this day.

Foreword

"All television is educational television. The question is: what is it teaching?"
—Nicholas Johnson, Former FCC Commissioner

We all try to teach our children that they should eat their vegetables, look both ways before crossing the street, and ultimately, discern right from wrong. We even send them off to school where they learn history, science, perhaps even physics. But who teaches the class *When to Use a Credit Card* or *How to Be Financially Responsible*? These lessons are all too often left in the hands of savvy marketers or worse yet, left solely up to chance and experience. In the world we live in, making one bad financial decision, just one, can have lasting effects for years and years to come.

The importance of knowing how to manage one's finances far too often does not come to light until one is in the dark hole of financial trouble.

The flip side of this scenario, though, is quite different. Imagine a situation where your children would have the knowledge, therefore the power, to not only manage their finances but to actually build true wealth. Even in a society that seems consumed with instant gratification, they would know that just because something is a good deal doesn't mean they should buy it. While we all teach our children to work hard, the lesson of teaching them how to make a dollar work for them can sometimes be elusive.

This book is meant not only to help you make your children smart about money but also wise. It is meant to plant the seeds of financial foresight that, with a little cultivation, can yield great things.

As you read this book, take the time to stop and discuss with your children not only the subject at hand but to share your own experiences and your own wisdom. It is the hope of the author and everyone involved with this project to give our children the insight and tools needed to be able to make well thought-out financial decisions.

—Kurt R. Opella
Managing Partner
LandMark Financial

Introduction

Facts are facts—truths are true. Truth is a force that is always in place, whether you are aware of it or not. The consequences associated with decisions based on the truth are real, whether you were aware of them or not. Take gravity, for instance. Gravity is the force that holds things on the planet. This is true whether you have studied about it or not. Even if you do not understand what the word means, gravity is the force that pulls dropped things back to the planet. Sometimes those things get broken. We learn to take care while carrying precious items and walking near precipices.

This book is about financial truths. It doesn't matter if you know the truths, believe them or not. These truths do not go away if you do not know about them or have the opinion that they do not apply to you. Uninformed decisions about spending money carry the same consequence as informed decisions. The money is spent. The difference between a good spending decision and a poor spending decision lies in when, how and what you spend your money on, and the costs associated with owning that item. Some decisions have really good consequences and some have very poor results.

It is my hope that after reading this book, you will ask your school principal to read it aloud to all classes, pass a copy along to a friend of any age, request city leaders and professionals to hold finance camps for people in your area, and that you will become committed to a building a solid financial future for yourself.

—Leann R. Voss
IYR, LLC

Chapter One

The twins were glum. Jared had broken his arm and was unable to attend basketball camp with his friends. Janae had fallen off the beam in gymnastics and she was out for the summer with a bad bruise.

When Dad walked in, both were surprised at his grin. "Hi, Dad, what's up?" asked Jared.

"Well, son, how would you and your sister like to attend Finance Camp for a few days?"

"Oh, boy! That sounds like fun!" exclaimed Janae.

Jared scowled. "It sounds like school to me," he said, frowning.

"Well, I'd like for you to understand why you are learning so many math facts in school, Jared. You needn't do sums, but this would sure help you know why your teachers spend so much time asking you to memorize addition and subtraction facts. Will you give it a try?"

"I'm ready, and Jared, it will beat sitting around here doing nothing. Mom doesn't let us watch much TV, and I am already tired of just reading books all the time. Aren't you?"

"That's right," Jared complained. "Mom hasn't let us play video games this summer any more than she does during school. Okay, Dad, but can I drop out if it starts

looking like school?" Jared's tone was joking, but he really meant it about school work.

"You bet," answered Dad. "I wouldn't want you having homework over the summer break!"

The next morning, as Dad was driving through town, Jared asked, "Where is this camp held, Dad?"

"Right here," Dad answered, as he parked the car.

Jared and Janae were surprised. They were at the bank!

Once inside, Dad introduced them to Mrs. Lewis. "I'll see you at lunch!" he said.

Mrs. Lewis led them across the big lobby. "How much about personal finances do you know?" she asked.

Janae said, "Well, Mom and Dad give us an allowance each week. They ask us to save some of our money so we will have spending money on trips we take when we are competing. Dad would like us to save as much as we can before we go to college."

"Yeah," said Jared, "Dad says he wants us to understand the value of the dollar, whatever that means."

"Keeping track of how your paycheck is spent is the foundation to building your net worth," said Mrs. Lewis.

"Paycheck?" repeated Janae.

"What's net worth?" asked Jared.

"That is what you are here at Finance Camp to find out," said Mrs. Lewis.

Mrs. Lewis led them into the bank's community room. There were other children from their neighborhood already seated. Jared and Janae were surprised. Each had assumed all the other kids from school were out of town at different camps. This would be a fun adventure after all!

"Let's get started," said Mrs. Lewis. "How much do receive when you are paid your allowance?"

"My mom gives me $5.00 each week after I finish my chores," said Tori.

"My dad gives me $7.00 after I mow the grass," said Dustin. "He used to give me $3.00 but since summer started and I mow, it's $7.00."

"You both used the word give but it would be more appropriate to substitute the word pay, since you perform a task and receive a certain amount in exchange for the finished chore," said Mrs. Lewis. "That could be called a wage, and wages become a paycheck at the end of the work week. Parents have used allowances for a long time to teach money management to their children."

"Wow," said Tori.

"How you manage your paycheck, along with your attitude about money and spending it, will determine your net worth," said Mrs. Lewis.

"What is net worth?" asked Jared, who was totally interested now. Jared liked to save his allowance, and rarely spent it on trips. "That is the second time I've heard that phrase."

"A person's net worth is the value of the assets owned minus the liabilities owed," answered Mrs. Lewis.

"I don't know what those words mean," said Tracy.

"Me, either," said Janae.

Mrs. Lewis drew a line down the middle of a sheet of paper. She titled one side "Assets" and the other side "Liabilities." Under the asset side she listed savings accounts, sports equipment, games and receivables (promises). On the other side she wrote debt (promises).

Financial Statement

Assets	Liabilities
Savings accounts	debt (promises)
Sports equipment	
Games	
Receivables (promises)	

She turned and said, "The word asset is a word we use to describe things like money or things that have a value."

"Things we like to have," said Jared.

"That's a good point, Jared. We all most generally like assets, if they are paid for! Liabilities are costs or promises to pay, called debt. We say we will do something and then we do it. During the time in between, when we have promised to do it, it is called a liability."

"You mean like waiting for my dad to pay me after I've mown the lawn?" Dustin asked.

"Yes, if he has offered to pay you $7.00 to mow the lawn and you have finished it, then he has a liability of $7.00 on his financial statement. You can list $7.00 on the asset side of *your* financial statement under 'promised,' or accounts receivable. When he pays you, you may deposit that money into your savings account and move that $7.00 listed as 'accounts receivable' to 'cash' on the asset side. Your dad's promise comes off of the liability section of his statement. Your dad subtracts $7.00 from his cash and the deal is done."

"Wow," said Jared, as he reached for a pencil. "I like that. I can calculate my weekly allowance until November 8th and I will know what my net worth will be on my birthday!"

"Watch out, Jared! You are doing math!" giggled his twin.

"I don't understand," said Tracy. "You have promises listed on both sides."

"Well," said Mrs. Lewis. "Promises can help us earn assets or lower our net worth. Learning to be careful with promises is a good lesson to learn."

"Why are promises so important?" asked Janae.

"Well, let's say that this afternoon a friend offers you a ticket to the movies this Friday night. You agree, or promise, to go with her. That is a good thing, going to a movie with a friend, right? Just like Dustin agreeing to mow the lawn. He'll earn $7.00. Remember, though, you owe time on Friday night to your friend. You are in debt.

"After dinner tonight, the phone rings and your mother answers. She relays this message to you: your favorite cousin from Wisconsin is coming for a visit. She and her family will be coming in on Friday afternoon and will spend the night. You are so excited...until you realize you have promised to go to the movie with a friend. You have already 'spent' that time by promising to attend a movie and that promise cost you the opportunity to visit with your cousin.

"You can call your friend and let her know what has happened. You may ask her if you can attend another time. If you have been careful with your promises, she will probably understand and invite you to come another time.

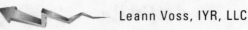

"But if you have been careless with your promises in the past, accepting too many offers and then backing out, your friend may stop inviting you along on trips. That feeling of not trusting you to keep your word to her becomes a real problem. The cost of broken promises may be higher than you want to pay. Promises are very important."

"But I thought this camp was about finances," said Jared, puzzled.

"It is," said Mrs. Lewis. "Finance is not just about addition and subtraction. It is about how well the assets and liabilities are managed, using accounting tools and ethics."

"Ethics?" chorused the group.

"Ethics," answered Mrs. Lewis. "Talk with your family tonight and we will discuss more tomorrow."

Chapter Two

"May we leave now?" asked Jared once more.

He had asked the question twice already. Janae was enjoying her toast and jam while Dad finished his coffee. Dad looked over the edge of his paper.

"What's this all about?"

"I'm just ready to get back to camp this morning," answered Jared. "I can't wait to find out more about finances."

"Any idea about what you'll be studying today?" asked Dad.

Jared sighed. "No. Mrs. Lewis just said to come with our thinking caps on today."

"Mrs. Lewis said we would be finding out about how the bank works," said Janae. "I hope we can see behind the teller windows."

"I don't want to study about how a bank works. I want to learn more about net worth and assets and stuff," grumbled Jared.

"Well, don't get too discouraged, Jared. There are two sides of personal finances—one dealing with managing assets and the other with building assets. Both areas are well worth studying."

"I really want to know how assets work, Dad. I hope Mrs. Lewis doesn't spend too much time introducing us to tellers we've known all our lives!"

Mrs. Lewis met the twins at the front entrance this morning. Tracy and Dustin were already waiting and Tori arrived just behind them.

"Sorry I am late, but I was still asking my grandmother questions," she said. "My grandmother is really hoping I learn about balancing something called a checkbook. She laughs and says she doesn't use checks much anymore, but she still has to balance her checkbook every month. Do you know what she is talking about, Mrs. Lewis?"

"Yes, I do and we are going to find out about that very subject right now," said Mrs. Lewis. "Let's go."

"That's more like it," said Jared.

Upstairs Mrs. Lewis introduced them to Mr. Stone.

"Hi, Mr. Stone," said Tori. "You worked at the concession stand for my sister's softball team fundraiser!"

"Yes, I did. Hello, everyone," said Mr. Stone.

"Mr. Stone oversees the accounting department of the bank. He will be showing you around the department this morning," said Mrs. Lewis. "I'll see you later."

"Do you use these machines to balance the checkbooks for everyone?" asked Tori. "My grandmother says it is one of the most important things she does each month."

"No, Tori. We use them to keep track of how much money each account has in it. Balancing the checkbook, or register, is the account owner's responsibility. Your grandmother is right that balancing her account is extremely important. However, these demand accounts are not just

for checks anymore," said Mr. Stone. "Lots of people use a debit card these days to pay for their purchases at the store. The card company gives the store credit and the total for the purchase is then debited, or subtracted, from the demand account at the time of the next upload."

"How long does that take?" asked Janae.

Mr. Stone replied, "Well, it depends on where the transaction occurs. It can be completed in just a few minutes, or it may take a couple of days. It shouldn't matter how long it takes, though, if you enter the amount in your register and subtract that amount from the total in your account."

Tracy asked, "What's a register?"

"Ah," said Mr. Stone, "I am glad you asked. Here is one for you to practice with while we talk.

							Starting Balance
Demand Account Register							
Check Number	Date	Payee/Transaction	Check Amount	•	Deposit Amount		$15.27
	29-Jun	paycheck -6-29			100.00		100.00
					Balance		115.27
	5-Jul	Hot Wire Electric	22.50				22.50
					Balance		92.77
					Balance		

"Let's say you've agreed to deposit your paycheck with us by direct deposit. Your company gave you a printout that shows $100.00 will be deposited today, June 29th."

"I've heard of direct deposit!" said Dustin. "Mom says it saves her from having to drop by the bank every Friday after she gets paid and standing in line to deposit her paycheck. She says she prefers to come home, get dinner started and to listen to what Tracy and I have been up to!"

"She also pays her bills online that evening," said Tracy. "Do you do that here, too?"

"Yes we do," said Mr. Stone. "Let's all bring our registers up to date. Please note that the registers I gave you show a balance in your account of $15.27. That's the beginning balance. Now note the $100.00 deposit and add that to your total. Here is a printout of a bill we need to pay, due on the 5th of July. If you were to go online to the bank's website to pay that bill, you would subtract, or deduct, from your register, $22.50. The bank would show the debit and subtract it from your account on the 5th."

"Dad says there are lots of different ways to pay bills these days, but Mom says she likes automatic payments best," said Jared. "How does that work?"

"Well, different companies have different forms and rules. Basically though, after you fill out the form, the company has permission to automatically, on a certain day, take out a specified amount of money from your account to pay a bill that happens regularly. Car payments, insurance premiums, utility bills and mortgage payments are examples of bills that come once a month. It is easy to get each one set up to be automatically taken from the account. It saves on time, paper and postage as well as helps the company have fewer runs to the bank with paper check deposits."

"Oh, I suppose Mom isn't the only one who would rather not have to stand in line!" said Tracy.

"Well," said Mr. Stone, "another good reason for Auto-mated Clearing House or ACH items is the time they can save for the businesses. Which would you rather do: pay someone to process payments, go to the bank, stand at the teller window, come back and file paper receipts, and then go back to processing payments, or pay your employee to process payments at a computer, finish the deposit trans-action with just a few computer key strokes and then go online to review it?"

"My dad would say it makes better sense to work it the ACH way," said Jared. "I can understand why he said finance camp would show me why I am learning to do arithmetic in school."

"He's right, Jared. Keeping up with the register of your account is one of the best ways I know of to keep track of your cash flow. It is the only way I know to pre-vent penalty fees from eating up your money and lowering your net worth," said Mr. Stone.

"Fees!" cried the group.

"Yes, fees," said Mr. Stone. "We are a business and we get paid for handling the accounts. We must keep our computer system up and running, pay the utility bills for the building, and we pay people to do all the account-ing. That is why there are often monthly fees for own-ing a demand account. There are also penalties for hav-ing insufficient funds in the account when a transaction occurs. The penalty fees are designed to discourage people from making transactions on their account when there is not enough money to pay for them. If a person makes a habit of making transactions without having the money in the account, that account may have to be closed. After that, it may be hard for that person to open another one."

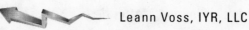

"Oh," said Jared, turning to his twin. "Now I understand what Dad meant last night when we talked. He said to practice ethical behavior is to act and maintain high standards of what you have been taught to know is right and good. Remember? He told us doing the right thing, even if no one sees or knows what is going on, is practicing good ethics. He said that what you earn is not as important as how well you manage it."

"This must be why he said there will be lots of times we will just need to do the right thing, even if we have to pass up opportunities," said his twin. "He said doing the right thing can seem hard sometimes."

Jared said slowly, "I guess keeping a checkbook up to date is ethical because if I don't, I may spend more than my paycheck is for the month."

"And if I don't have the money in my account to pay for it, it is like stealing," said Janae.

"That's right, Janae," said Mr. Stone. "You should never write a check or authorize a transaction for more than is in your account."

"No wonder Mother tells me all the time to practice my math skills so I will do better," said Janae. "Now I know why."

Chapter Three

"Buckle up, everyone," said Mrs. Lewis.

"Where are we going?" asked Tori from the back of the van.

"We are going to meet someone today who will explain contracts and how they affect us," explained Mrs. Lewis. "Someone who looks at contracts all the time is called an attorney-at-law or a lawyer."

"Wow," said Janae. "I've always wanted to meet a lawyer."

"Why?" asked Tracy.

"Well, they always solve crimes and show who really stole the money when I watch them on television. I think they would be really smart."

"Here we are," said Mrs. Lewis.

"Wow," said Janae.

Inside, the children were led to a room with a big, long, wooden table that had lots of chairs around it. The children sat down and looked around at all the books on shelves that lined the wall on one side. There were hundreds of bound books that were very thick.

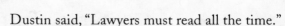
Dustin said, "Lawyers must read all the time."

"Not so much out of books anymore, but we do read a lot from the Internet these days," answered a cheerful voice from the doorway.

All the children spun around in surprise. They recognized the voice as that of Mr. McCalla, their Youth Association soccer coach.

"Wow," said Janae, with a look of disbelief on her face. "I didn't know you solved crimes."

"No, Janae, I don't solve crimes. But I do try to help people avoid problems that could lead to unpleasant circumstances."

"What do you mean?" asked Jared.

"Well, Jared, contracts are agreements, verbal or written, between people and those agreements are enforceable by law. Contracts are the basis of financial transactions. There could not be financial transactions without contracts," answered Mr. McCalla.

Tori spoke up. "Would you give me an example of a contract that is a financial transaction, Mr. McCalla?"

"I can name one easily. The demand accounts at the bank you learned about are really good examples of contracts. A check, debit card, or any other transaction requires a customer and a bank that is legally chartered to do business. In order for a bank to do business, it must agree to follow certain legal guidelines and rules. A customer opening an account will read the terms of the contract, which states how transactions are handled, what the customer can or cannot do, and also what the bank can or cannot do. If the customer agrees to the terms and signs the contract, the bank will open the account. That account will remain open as long as both parties do what they have

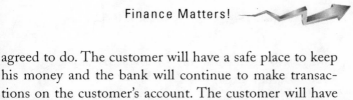

agreed to do. The customer will have a safe place to keep his money and the bank will continue to make transactions on the customer's account. The customer will have access to check writing, debit card, online and other privileges as long as he keeps his word concerning his account contract."

"So the penalty fees that Mr. Stone told us about are part of a contract?" Janae wondered out loud. "Is that why we should keep track in our registers?"

"Yes, indeed," said Mr. McCalla. "Penalty fees are a contractual way of saying 'You are not keeping your promise' and are usually effective in helping people understand they have done something wrong. When fees are charged, people may feel angry because their mistake cost them money, but paying the money helps them realize how important it is to keep their part of the contract."

"What is a contract exactly?" asked Jared.

"Contracts are agreements that give what is called consideration and benefit to both parties, but each party must keep his word or the agreed upon penalties will be enforced," answered Mr. McCalla.

"Let's suppose Jared contracts with me to mow my lawn this year. Our terms are on each Saturday, for twelve weeks, Jared agrees to be finished mowing my lawn by four o'clock p.m. and I agree to pay him $15.00. The terms also include a section that states if Jared doesn't finish until 6:00 pm, he will be paid only $12.00 that week and this can happen only two times in one summer. If Jared is late finishing my yard a third time, the contract is broken, and I can find another person to mow my yard. This contract assures Jared that, in exchange for twelve Saturdays of mowing my yard on time, he will earn $180,

and it also assures me my yard will be mowed on time each Saturday all summer."

"Oh, I see," said Tori, turning to Mrs. Lewis. "The checking account has rules about how many times a person can make mistakes in the checkbook."

"Yes, there are rules about the demand accounts at the bank," Mrs. Lewis said. "If a customer doesn't take care of the account, the contract says there will be fees assessed and the account may have to be closed."

"Mrs. Lewis, have you explained about the rules concerning interest?" asked Mr. McCalla.

"No, not yet," answered Mrs. Lewis.

"What is interest?" chorused the children.

"Wait and see!" said Mrs. Lewis mysteriously.

Chapter Four

"Where would you like to eat lunch?" asked Mrs. Lewis.

"Market Fresh Stir-Fry!" shouted the children.

"Okay!" replied Mrs. Lewis.

Jared and Janae were on another Finance Camp adventure. Sometimes Mrs. Lewis would not tell them where they were going or who they would meet, but the children always looked forward to the outings. They were learning about banking and contracts while visiting with professionals in their town. Dad had been right, Jared admitted to himself. Dad had known all along that Jared was keenly interested in learning more about money and how to build his net worth.

As Mrs. Lewis pulled into the restaurant parking lot, the children grew silent in their anticipation. This was going to be a fun experience! As they got out of the van, they spotted a familiar face.

"Hey, Mr. Plummer!" said Tracy. "I haven't seen you since our Cancer Awareness Walk!"

"It's good to see you again, Tracy. Hello," said Mr. Plummer to the rest of the group. "I've been expecting you."

"But Mrs. Lewis just asked us where we wanted to go while we were in the van!" exclaimed Dustin in surprise.

"Mrs. Lewis told me she would ask where you wanted to go for lunch," answered Mr. Plummer. "I thought you would choose this restaurant. In fact, I would've been surprised if you hadn't chosen this one. Let's go in. They have a big table saved for us."

The children looked around in awe as the hostess led them to their table. The business had just opened this week, and the children were amazed they were actually going to eat here. Even more surprising was the fact that Mr. Plummer was their host.

"But you are a famous radio announcer," protested Tracy after they had been seated. "What does that have to do with net worth or finances?"

"And how could you guess we would be coming here to eat?" demanded Jared.

"Well, the fact that I could guess where you would want to eat is based on the fact that I work in radio and I pay attention to marketing," answered Mr. Plummer.

"What is marketing?" asked Janae.

"Ah, Janae, that is a good question! Have you ever eaten at a Market Fresh Stir-Fry?"

"No," answered Janae. "But I've seen it on TV."

"Has anyone here eaten at a Market Fresh Stir-Fry restaurant?" Mr. Plummer asked the rest of the group. "No? But how did you know about it? What made you want to choose to eat here?"

Dustin replied, "My cousin ate at one while he was away at a tournament. He said it was really fun to choose what was cooked and eating with the chop sticks was interesting. He also said the food is served in really cool bowls."

"My sister said that choosing the vegetables was great. She said it was the best way to eat she had ever tried," added Tori.

Jared and Janae both admitted to reading about it on the Internet after their mother had told them about the restaurant being built here.

"Mom said that people are really interested in eating more healthy foods and that the restaurant employees were people who understood the Food Guide Pyramid. She said they could explain how the nutrients in the foods help our bodies grow and develop," said Janae.

"Yeah, Mom and Dad are really interested in the environment and locally grown foods," added Jared.

"Sounds like successful marketing to me," said Mr. Plummer. "Your cousin, Dustin, and your sister, Tori, have informed others about Market Fresh Stir-Fry by what is called "word of mouth." It is a testimonial form-sharing with others from a personal experience. Jared and Janae, you and your parents have heard about it through the media-television and radio advertisements, newspaper and internet stories. These are all examples of marketing. Marketing is the way a business presents itself in order to get the message across and that message is almost invariably 'buy this,' 'you cannot do without this' or 'try it.' In this case, Market Fresh Stir-Fry has done a pretty good job, don't you think?"

"I guess so," answered Janae, "but I still don't understand how you knew we would come here for lunch."

"Well, I watch TV and we run commercials at the radio station, so I knew this place was opening this week. I thought all of you might have seen or heard the commercials and would know it was open. Am I right?"

All the children nodded.

"I also thought that since your parents are pretty health conscious they might have mentioned they thought this would be a good place to try sometime. Am I right?"

Again all the children nodded.

"And the last thing that told me you might choose this place is the reputation this chain has. Choosing your own fresh ingredients, including fresh herbs and spices, then watching as it is stir fried and served up in these special bowls looks fun. I thought that might sway you, if given a chance to eat here. Was I right?"

"Yes!" said the children.

Mr. Plummer said, "It seems to me, then, that the Market Fresh Stir-Fry marketing department has done its job well. The company has spent money touting this restaurant through popular advertising means; television, radio, print and Internet ads. People who earn money and make spending decisions, consumers like your parents and family members, have decided to try this place and have told others they like it."

Jared was amazed. "Are you telling me that marketing is a business to make commercials and the whole purpose is to try to get me to spend my money a certain way?"

"Yes, generally speaking," said Mr. Plummer. "Commercials let people know what is for sale, like the food at this restaurant. Their commercials have worked. The business has grown, built more restaurants, and Wall Street has said the stock value looks good."

"Wall Street? Where is that? And what is stock value?"

Mrs. Lewis spoke up. "Let's get our food and talk some more later!"

"Please!" said Janae. "I am really ready to try this out."

"Me, too!" said Tori.

"Then let's go," said Mr. Plummer.

Chapter Five

"I really wish you would call him this morning," said Mom. "It makes me nervous having to use it, even to run short errands."

Jared and Janae looked at each other. They had not heard Mom use that tone of voice before. But even more surprising was Dad's answer!

"I'll take Jared and Janae with me this morning and we will see what we can do. But we are only shopping! Jared! Jan…Oh, there you are. Would you like to come with me this morning?"

Jared and Janae rounded the corner and answered breathlessly, "Yes!"

Dad opened the door for them and called out to Mom, "We'll be back later. We won't be in for lunch, though."

Janae couldn't hold back her questions as she walked to the car. "Where are we going, Dad?"

"We are off to make your mom happy today," answered Dad mysteriously.

"What is it that makes Mom nervous?" questioned Jared.

"I'll answer your questions later," said Dad, "but first I want to ask you some questions about Finance Camp. Can you tell me about some of the things you have learned?"

"Well, we haven't really talked about net worth a whole lot. I really was interested in that. We spent a lot of time talking to Mr. Stone about keeping track of accounts. That's the reason we have to learn how to do math at school," said Jared.

"Mrs. Lewis has talked to us about financial statements and ethics. She took us to see Mr. McCalla. Did you know he is an attorney?" asked Janae.

"Yes, he has been my attorney for years," said Dad.

Jared was surprised. "You have an attorney?" he asked. "Why?"

"Oh, he helped us when we moved here and bought our house several years ago. Your mother and I asked him to draw up a contract when we sold that house. He also helped us set up our trusts two or three years ago."

"Trusts?" asked Janae. "What is a trust?"

"Oh, Janae, we are here. May I answer your question later?" asked Dad as he pulled into the bank parking lot.

"Sure," she said, "but why are we at the bank?"

"I want to talk to Mr. Koehler," answered Dad. "Then we may go shopping."

Once inside the lobby, a tall man strode over to Dad. As the men shook hands, Dad introduced the twins. Janae and Jared giggled and Mr. Koehler explained.

"I met Jared and Janae a couple of years ago while teaching a savings program at the Grand Avenue School," said Mr. Koehler. He turned to the twins. "I seem to remember the two of you coming in to open savings accounts after we finished those classes. I was happy to see you have been attending Finance Camp with Mrs. Lewis."

He turned to Dad. "What can I do for you today?" he asked.

"Well," said Dad, "the old van has been acting up lately and we need to repair it. I thought I would drop in and ask you how much it may be worth and what I may be able to spend on a replacement."

"Oh, boy!" gasped Jared out loud.

Janae's jaw dropped.

"Good idea," said Mr. Koehler, smiling widely. "Let's go to my office."

Later, when Mr. Koehler had looked it up on his computer, he told Dad what the old van might be worth if Dad chose to sell it and what the trade in value might be. Dad mentioned a few ideas about makes and models of vans, thanked him and told Mr. Koehler he would be in touch.

Jared was really fired up now. "I think Mom would like a red one," he said as they left Mr. Koehler's office.

"Will we get to take it home today?" Janae wondered.

"Right now we have another stop to make," answered Dad. He headed across the lobby and up the stairs. He stepped into an office in the far corner and asked, "Have you got a minute?"

The man sitting behind the desk stood up and shook Dad's hand. "Yes, anytime. Who have you got with you?"

"These are my twin children. Jared and Janae, this is Mr. Molder," said Dad.

"It is nice meeting you, Mr. Molder," said Jared. "Haven't I seen you at the gym with the wrestlers?"

"Yes you have, Jared. It is fun helping the coach out during the season and helps me keep in shape," answered Mr. Molder.

Mr. Molder invited them to sit down. "What can I do for you today?" he asked.

Dad said, "I am thinking of replacing our older van and wondered what the premium might be for a replacement."

While Mr. Molder looked at his computer, Jared asked Dad, "What is a premium?"

"Ah," said Mr. Molder, "I guess Mrs. Lewis hasn't covered that yet, has she, in Finance Camp?"

"No," said Janae. "Your business card says insurance. What is insurance?"

"Insurance may be defined as a contract between an owner of a tangible thing of value, like a car, house, or boat and a company specializing in risk. The company does a lot of research, analyzing how many accidents happen to each kind of those things over time. Based on that research, the company writes a contract which agrees to replace or repair the item of value if an accident destroys or damages it and charges an amount, called premium, to the customer," answered Mr. Molder.

"Are you an attorney, like Mr. McCalla?" asked Janae.

"No. A person does not have to be an attorney to sell insurance contracts; however, a person who sells insurance must be licensed in each state they sell insurance business in. It is a regulated business.

"If you want to keep the same coverage, it looks as though your premium would go up about $17.50 to $23.75 a month. It depends on what make and model you decide on," said Mr. Molder to Dad.

"Thanks," said Dad. "I'll let you know."

Later, Dad bought sandwiches and milk and took the twins to the park. During lunch, Jared asked, "Dad, why did we spend all morning talking to people instead of looking at vans? It is a lot of work and really isn't all that fun."

Janae disagreed. "I liked getting to meet everyone, Dad. It was fun. But I thought you said you were going to get a van for Mom."

"I did say I would go shopping, but I did not say I would necessarily be buying!" Dad laughed. "The reason I have made so many stops this morning and wanted you to be with me is so you will understand that purchasing a vehicle isn't as easy as it sounds. Car commercials make it *seem* as though all you must do is come in and choose the car you'd like to drive."

"That's marketing," said Janae. "Mr. Plummer explained that marketing sets up the commercials to let us know how our money can be spent. Companies selling products or services spend a lot of money trying to get our attention so we will want to buy what they are selling."

"That's right," said Dad. "And they know how to do a good job, too! I saw a really nice van your mother would like to drive, but, as you have seen today, I must think about the impact of my purchase *before* I buy anything."

"What do you mean?" asked Jared.

"Well, Mr. Koehler told me how much I can expect to get for our old van, whether I trade it in or sell it. That means I would need to write a check for the difference to pay for a new one or apply for a loan. A loan would make the van cost even more to buy. Mr. Molder said the premium for a new van would cost more each month and..."

"You have to pay a premium now?" asked Janae.

"Yes, each vehicle your mother and I own has an insurance premium we pay each month," answered Dad.

"Why do you have insurance? Why can't you just buy a car?" asked Jared, who was puzzled.

"Well, insurance protects my investment in my car,

protects other cars if I cause an accident and protects my net worth," explained Dad. "It is another contractual part of finance. Some folks borrow money to buy their cars. A loan contract may state the person must have insurance on the car to protect the collateral, or thing of value the loan is for. If the car is hurt in an accident, the contract states the insurance company will help pay to fix it back. This protects the loan. If I own the car outright, I can choose an insurance contract that protects my car and the other car, if I damage someone else's car in an accident. The insurance will help pay for repairs, so the insurance contract protects my net worth."

"Oh," said Jared. He did not sound convinced.

Dad added, "Mom and I also have insurance on our things in our house, like furniture, pictures and computers."

"You mean my video games are insured?" asked Jared.

"Yes," said Dad. "Your mom and I work hard to earn our income. We have paid for those things, along with our cars. We may not like having to pay premiums each month for something we cannot see or enjoy, but we do pay them so we can protect our net worth."

"I'm done with my sandwich," said Janae.

"So am I," said Dad. "Jared, if you are ready, we will go."

"Are we going to pick out a van for Mom?" asked Janae.

"Well, I need to stop by the Department of Motor Vehicles," answered Dad. "I need to find out how much the license plate tax will cost."

"You have to pay tax on a car?" asked Jared. He and Janae were incredulous.

"Let's get into the car and I'll explain," answered Dad.

Chapter Six

"Hey Dad, when are you going to buy a van?" asked Jared as the twins headed out the door.

"Well, Jared, your mother and I have not made up our minds yet," answered Dad. "There are a lot of things that we are considering right now and a van is not a priority."

"Oh," said Jared, disappointment in his tone. "I was really looking forward to shopping for a new one with you."

"Well, nothing says we can't shop!" said Dad, laughing. "But depreciation can have a lot to do with what I choose to buy!"

"What's depreciation?" asked Janae as Jared repeated the new word.

"Depreciation may be described as the loss of value of an item over time," answered Dad. "Depreciation is a destroyer of net worth. Ask Mrs. Lewis. See if she doesn't know someone who can explain it a little bit better."

"Thanks, Dad," said Jared, as they pulled up to the bank.

"We'll see you after camp," said Janae.

Once inside the bank, the children made their way across the lobby. As they were walking along, Jared was

very thoughtful. When he spotted Mrs. Lewis, he said, "What is depreciation?"

"Ah, Jared, you have been visiting with your father again, haven't you? You are always asking questions!"

"Well, Dad said depreciation destroys net worth, and I want to make sure I know what it is."

"Well, you are in luck! Today we are going to visit with a person who can answer all your questions. Isn't that right, Mr. Johnston?" said Mrs. Lewis as she shook hands with a man stepping off the elevator.

"Well, I am not sure about that," chuckled Mr. Johnston, "but I can answer some questions! Hello, Jared. Janae, it is nice to see you here."

Janae looked up at Mr. Johnston in surprise. "But you teach basketball at the Y!"

"I do," said Mr. Johnston, "but only after I get off work. I am an accountant when I'm not coaching hoops at the YMCA!"

"I didn't know that," said Janae, amazed.

"Let's have a seat and get started today," said Mrs. Lewis. "Tracy, Tori, have you met Mr. Johnston? I know you have, Dustin."

"Yes, ma'am, we have," answered Tracy as Tori replied, "Yes, his team beat us in a tournament a few weeks ago! Come coach us!"

"Thanks!" said Mr. Johnston. "You played a really good game, but the real reason I am here today is to help you understand a principle. It is called depreciation and it is important to realize depreciation is always at work when dealing with finances. Depreciation works in close association with marketing, and these two principles, if not understood well by consumers, can wreak havoc on net worth."

"What are consumers?" asked Dustin.

Mr. Johnston grinned. "I would say any person who spends money for anything, actually, for things sold in a department store, grocery store, car lot, restaurant, online web pages, anywhere, that person is a consumer!"

"My dad said today he might not buy a car because of depreciation. He said it could destroy net worth. How could that happen?" asked Jared.

"Well, your dad is correct. Let's set up a financial statement here. Do you know what a financial statement is?"

"Yes," said Dustin. "It is a list of things you own with the value listed to one side and the other side lists things you promised to do, but haven't finished yet."

"That is a great explanation," said Mr. Johnston, "and those promised things on this side are called liabilities."

As he was speaking, Mr. Johnston drew a financial statement on the board. He asked each camper to name one asset and as he listed them, he gave each asset a value in dollars.

"No financial statement is complete without a listing of the dollar value of the asset," he said. "This is where the tricky principle of depreciation comes in. Dustin, you had me list a bicycle here as your asset. I do not know what you paid for the bike, but for today's purpose, I am going to assign the value of a new bike on this financial statement as $100.00. Tracy, the value I am going to assign new ice skates will be $100.00, as will Tori's basketball. Janae, your movie and Jared's bat will each be valued at $100.00. We will use a hypothetical price of $100.00 for each item.

"I am totaling these items up and the value is $500.00. We'll list them as presents newly received, so we will list nothing on the liabilities side. The financial statement gives a net worth of..."

"...of five hundred dollars," finished a chorus of voices.

Financial Statement		
Assets		Liabilities
Bicycle	100.00	Debt (promises)
Ice skates	100.00	
Basketball	100.00	
DVD movie	100.00	
Bat	100.00	
Total	$500.00	$-0-

"Yes," said Mr. Johnston, "this client has a net worth of five hundred dollars on, say, January first. Okay?"

"Okay," answered the group.

"Now, what happens when our client takes his ball out of the cardboard box and down the street to play with his friends? It gets scuffed, right? We all know this is what happens. It isn't bad, just the normal wear-and-tear of playing basketball. The same thing happens when the skates are worn to practice, the bike is ridden and the bat gets used in a game. The principle of depreciation is at work here, though. A basketball is no longer new, skates get scuffed, the bike gets a scratch and the DVD is opened to play the movie. We buy the things to use but, over time, they become more and more worn. The cash value we assign to them next year would be less. When we look at the list, what can we say the used basketball's value would be compared to a new ball? Fifty dollars? Okay. How about the skates? Could we buy them second hand for $80? Okay, we'll list that here. What about the bat? Maybe $65? The bike might retain more value, so we assign it a value of $90. And lastly, the DVD. It may have been your favorite movie last year, but it may only be worth $20 now if we were to put it up for sale.

First Year		
Assets		Liabilities
Bicycle	100.00	Debt (promises)
Ice skates	100.00	
Basketball	100.00	
DVD movie	100.00	
Bat	100.00	
Total	$500.00	$-0-

Second Year		
Assets		Liabilities
Bicycle	90.00	Debt (promises)
Ice skates	80.00	
Basketball	50.00	
DVD movie	20.00	
Bat	65.00	
Total	$305.00	$-0-

"Let's see. Depreciation took a lot of value from our list of consumer goods. Our client's net worth is down from $500 to $305. That is quite a hit, isn't it, especially since it is only after the first year," said Mr. Johnston.

"Whoa!" exclaimed Jared. "I am never buying anything again!"

"That is not the point I am trying to make, Jared," said Mr. Johnston. "The point is to decide to make purchases after you have given some thought to the consequences. Mr. Plummer talked with you about marketing earlier, and while advertising does serve the purpose to let you know what you could purchase with your money, it also is designed to get you to spend your money without thinking about how it can affect your net worth. Keeping the goal of building your net worth can help you make good spending decisions your whole life. That goal is a personal responsibility, though. No one can make you choose to spend wisely."

"But if everything loses value after you've bought it, how can you build net worth?" asked Janae.

"Ah, what an excellent question!" said Mr. Johnston. "If you have a plan and a budget, and learn to think about purchases, you will develop the habit of spending for quality purchases that keep their value over a longer period of time. This habit will serve you well as you grow older and begin earning wages. Understanding when to buy something may be as important as deciding what to buy, in the long run."

"Does everything we buy depreciate?" asked Tracy.

"There are some exceptions to the rule, Tracy, like works of art or other valuable collectibles and real estate, which are valued by professionals on formal written forms called appraisals. Generally speaking though, yes, all consumer goods depreciate," answered Mr. Johnston. "Cars are so well known for depreciation there are businesses totally dedicated to keeping a tally of what the value is for each type of car made each year and the current value for older makes and models. Buying a car is not as easy as it may seem."

"I know," said Jared sadly. "I really thought my dad would buy one, but I don't think he will now."

"There are lots of commercials advertising new ones all the time. Remember, there will be new cars for sale next year and the ones sold today lose a lot of value to depreciation, so in some cases, it may be a better deal to wait. There are lots of good reasons to take time to think spending decisions over. Today I've shown you one good reason. There are many others."

"Bye, Mr. Johnston," said Janae. "I'll see you at the Y."

"Mrs. Lewis?"

"Yes, Jared."

"I have a question."

"Let's go to lunch, Jared, and maybe afterward we'll find the answer!" said Mrs. Lewis.

Chapter Seven

After lunch, the children were surprised to find several new video games on display in the community room at the bank. When asked what they were for, Mrs. Lewis replied mysteriously, "Wait and see!"

Dustin and Jared stood in front of the monitor with the sport bikes. Dustin said, "I have seen this game played at my friend's house. His brother has it. It is cool the way the graphics spray the dirt as the bikes take the corners!"

Jared replied, "I watched my cousins play during the holidays, but I have never played it."

Meanwhile, the girls hovered near another game set displaying several different avatars walking through a virtual town. "Look at how realistically their fingers move…" said Tracy.

"Hello," said a cheerful voice. The children turned to find a small woman in the doorway. "I am Mrs. Duke," she said, introducing herself. "I am a loan officer with the bank. May I find out your names?"

Dustin exclaimed, "I saw you slicing watermelons at the Watermelon Festival!"

"Yes, you did!" agreed Mrs. Duke. "We had a lot of people come for watermelon. It was fun!"

After the children introduced themselves, Jared asked the question everyone wanted to ask, "What are the games for?"

"Well, I wanted to talk to you about consumer purchases this afternoon," Mrs. Duke answered. "They can affect your net worth more than you realize."

"Mr. Johnston explained that this morning," said Jared. "But I guess I didn't realize he meant buying games like this. There are all sorts of things you can do with them, and new versions come out all the time. My cousins bought one."

"Was it the new football joystick? That one will let you decide if the punt will be a soccer style kick or a straight away style!"

"Yes, that is it! How did you know?" asked Jared, amazed.

"Marketing! I have watched those commercials and figured you have, too. All the folks who produce and sell these machines really hope you have!" answered Mrs. Duke. "Do you know how much these new sets cost?"

"Over half my allowance for the year!" said Tori. "I do not think I will ever have one."

"Tori, I'm glad you mentioned that. Would you stand up that card laying there in front of that machine? It lists the cost of the setup with the avatars and the ability to move them around with a keyboard. See, $120.00. Now to upgrade it with the joystick would cost $45.00 more. It costs a total of $165.00."

"But the card says $199.00," protested Tracy.

"Ah," said Mrs. Duke. "You have discovered hidden costs."

"What do you mean by 'hidden costs?'" asked Janae.

"Do you know about sales tax?" asked Mrs. Duke.

"Yes," answered Tracy. "There are sales taxes on most things you buy. That isn't hidden."

"Have you calculated the tax for the game? The tax rate is 8.75%," said Mrs. Duke as she handed out calculators. She added, "The easiest way to calculate tax is to multiply the cost times 1.0875. That way you include the cost and only have one calculation to make."

"That total is only $179.44," said Tori. "What else is hidden?"

"The cost for taking a year to pay for it," answered Mrs. Duke. "Do you see the print there?" Mrs. Duke pointed out some fine print along the bottom of the sign. "The total is $199.00."

Jared thought hard and asked, "It costs $20.00 for time?"

"Yes, Jared. Time, in financial terms, is called interest. If you buy something on time, you pay interest. The interest here was calculated at a rate of 21% for one year."

Tracy said, "Wow! That added a lot to the price."

Mrs. Duke answered, "Yes, it did."

She turned to Tori. "How much is your weekly allowance?"

Tori answered, "$5.00."

"Well, Tori, if you were to agree to the terms of this contract, you would have to pay $3.83 each week to the store. That would leave only $1.17 each week for a whole year for you to save or spend for your other needs.

"Many times shoppers who have seen a lot of advertising can forget to calculate the true cost of something they want. It is easy to sign a contract, take home something new and exciting, then forget about paying for it until the bill arrives in the mail. Often, when a credit card bill comes, there is not enough money in the checking account to pay for it entirely. That is how a hidden cost like interest can make a $179.44 item end up costing $199.00. Sometimes, when credit card contracts allow a loan to reach a very high total, the payment each month posts only a few dollars to item cost and many dollars to interest. That type of interest can make an item that originally cost $200.00 end up costing $300, $400 or more."

"I do not understand," said Tracy. "How do you buy something without having the money to pay for it?"

"Well, Tracy, it used to work like this," explained Mrs. Duke. "Because a loan from the bank was a lot of work for small purchases, many stores used to offer in-store credit. A customer charged what was needed or wanted throughout the month, traditionally starting on the first of the month. An employee, usually a bookkeeper, would add up the total for that month and mail the bill out on the first day of the next month. Payment in full was expected by the tenth. If the check for payment arrived late, say after the twentieth, a late fee would be added to the next month's bill.

"But most stores no longer pay employees to calculate a store bill. Instead, they have a credit card machine. Customers see signs on the door as they walk in the business. These signs tell them whether or not a card is accepted."

"How do those work? Our mom has a credit card. She pays for everything she buys at the store with it because she likes to pay only one bill each month. She says it is easier to account for her purchases when she balances her checkbook," said Dustin.

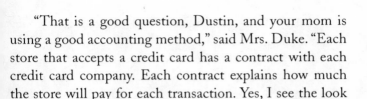

"That is a good question, Dustin, and your mom is using a good accounting method," said Mrs. Duke. "Each store that accepts a credit card has a contract with each credit card company. Each contract explains how much the store will pay for each transaction. Yes, I see the look on your face, Jared. It is surprising.

"The store has to pay to have the card machine at the register. Some contracts charge a certain percent for each transaction and some charge a flat fee. Each contract specifies when the credit card company will deposit the money from each sale into the business's account. This keeps the business from having to go the bank all the time to make deposits.

"Your mother and the businesses who accept credit cards have passed the chore of bookkeeping to credit card companies. The business charges a little more for each item it sells to cover the fees for accepting the cards and concentrates on stocking or producing goods and services.

"The credit card companies also keep each customer's account current and up to date. For that service, the credit card company often charges an annual fee to each customer. Then, each month, a statement of what was spent goes to each customer. The customer can choose to pay it all at the end of the month and avoid paying interest, like your mother, Dustin. The customer may choose to pay only part of what is owed. These options are listed in the contract.

"If the customer decides to pay only part of the bill, the unpaid portion of the bill becomes consumer debt, or a credit card loan. Interest is calculated on the oldest part of the unpaid amount and is included in the new unpaid

balance. The next statement issued will reflect that new balance and any new purchase details."

"Mrs. Duke, that sounds very complicated," said Janae.

"It is very complicated and can become very expensive," said Mrs. Duke.

She continued, "Let's suppose I charge $2,000.00 on my credit card and that credit card carries 21% interest. Let's also suppose that I only have $50.00 a month to spend to pay off the balance. It could take about seventy months, that is 5 years and 10 months, to finish paying that money back. $50 dollars times 70 equals $3,500. That is spending an extra $1,500 for the use of someone else's money for almost 6 years. And I haven't even charged anything else.

"You see, time can cost a lot of money. A whole lot of money. You would be wise to remember the old adage about a free ... "

"Lunch!" chorused Jared and Janae.

"But how do you know that?" asked Mrs. Duke, looking surprised.

"Our dad, he says it all the time. He says he can't find a free lunch. He says someone pays,'" answered Janae.

"Yes, he told me just last night that there were many things that looked good but after they are bought, can be really hard to take care of," Jared said glumly. "He said it about a new car."

"Oh, I see," said Mrs. Duke. "Balancing the family budget can be tricky and parents sometimes would like to have new things. But making sure that their net worth increases each year is the most important priority. It does make saying no to yourself and your family more difficult, though."

"Mrs. Duke, how does interest lower your net worth?" asked Dustin.

"Well," she said as she turned to the financial statement. "Let's revise this statement you worked on with Mr. Johnston. Let's suppose you *bought* all these things on January 1st. Let's also suppose you bought them on credit. You'll pay, with tax...how much? Thanks, Jared, you'll pay $543.75 for the goods. Remember, they are only worth $500.00, though.

"Now let me show you the amount you would pay for one year to borrow that $543.75. I brought this to show you. At the end of a year, at 21% interest, it would cost $603.72. The interest, or cost of time to pay it out, is $59.97. Okay, we list the liability for these assets worth $500.00 while they are still new and in the box, unopened, at $603.72. We valued them at $305.00 at the end of the year, so after one year, we have paid over $600 for something that is worth only about half that amount just as we finish paying it off.

First Year			
Assets		**Liabilities**	
Bicycle	100.00	Sporting Goods Loan	543.75
Ice skates	100.00		
Basketball	100.00	(interest payable)	59.97
DVD movie	100.00		
Bat	100.00		
Total	$500.00		$603.72

Second Year			
Assets		**Liabilities**	
Bicycle	90.00	Debt (promises)	
Ice skates	80.00		
Basketball	50.00		
DVD movie	20.00		
Bat	65.00		
Total	$305.00		$-0-

"When credit is used, the fact that you are paying more than the asking price coupled with the depreciation of the good that was bought makes most goods cost a lot more than most people realize. Sometimes consumers are not aware that paying for goods over a long period of time by paying only minimum payments can make the actual cost skyrocket. Interest can turn credit card purchases into huge loans and the original items bought may be broken or consumed well before the loan is paid off. The loan shows up here, on the liabilities side. The goods are listed here, but at the depreciated value as time goes by. If the loan is for a service then there would be nothing to list on the asset side. And, if the goods bought were groceries or tickets to last week's game, there would be nothing at all to list on the asset side."

"Wow," said Tori. "That doesn't look good."

Tracy nodded. "I think I will visit my friend and play with her game."

"Yes," said Jared. "This building net worth takes a lot of thought."

Just then Mrs. Lewis stepped into the room. "Thank you, Mrs. Duke, for explaining about consumer debt today. We appreciate it."

She turned to Janae and Jared. "Your parents are waiting to pick you up. Would you meet them in the lobby?"

"Oh, boy!" exclaimed Jared. "Come on, Janae! I'll bet we're going to get a new van!"

Chapter Eight

Jared and Janae wondered what was up. Mom and Dad had asked them to hop in the van but wouldn't tell the twins where they were going.

"Janae, are you buckled up?" asked Mom.

"Yes, I am now," answered Janae, "but couldn't I have a hint?"

"No, Janae, and don't think Jared was able to pry it from Dad, either!" replied Mom, laughing. "You will just have to wait and see!"

"I think we are getting a van!" whispered Jared to Janae as he got in. "Dad is really excited and was talking to Mr. Koehler in the lobby just now. He said it was just what they had been looking for and that Mom loved it the first time they saw it."

"I wonder what color it is?" mused Janae.

A few minutes later Jared was disappointed when Dad pulled up into a driveway. This was a neighborhood he was not familiar with. He didn't hear what Mom said as he and Janae got out, but was really surprised when Dad said, "Yes, I think a maple tree planted by the front door would be lovely," to Mom.

"Mrs. Howell, it's good to see you!" Dad's voice rang out a greeting to a very familiar figure walking up the drive. It was Mrs. Howell, a reading mentor from their old school.

"And it is good to see you again. Jared, Janae, I hope you are enjoying your summer vacation," said Mrs. Howell.

"Yes we are," answered Janae. "Do you live here?"

"No, I don't," said Mrs. Howell. "But would you like to see the house?"

Jared was really confused now, and Janae was, too. Mom and Dad turned to the twins and Dad said, "How would you like to move to this house? Mom and I want to buy it!"

"Wow," breathed Janae and Jared let out a shout. "Would I? Yes!"

Once inside, the twins instantly loved the place. Mrs. Howell, Mom and Dad showed them the house, and the twins decided which rooms would be theirs. When they got back downstairs, Janae asked when they would be moving.

"We'll be closing in August. The movers will be at our old house the day before we close to get things ready to go," answered Mom.

"Closing? What does that mean?" Jared wondered out loud and Janae exclaimed, "We have to wait a month before we can move in?"

Mrs. Howell said, "Do you remember visiting with Mr. McCalla during Finance Camp?"

"Yes, I do," answered Janae.

"Did he explain that financial contracts protect people as they conduct business?"

"Yes, he said contracts were the basis for transactions," said Jared, "but he didn't say anything about houses."

"Well," explained Mrs. Howell, "generally when a house is bought or sold, there are many contracts to be

signed. There are inspections of the property and valu-
ations that must be performed. A complete history of
transactions on the real estate must be prepared for attorneys to examine and financial details like paying taxes,
eliminating liens, buying insurance and applying for loans
must be completed before the closing or title transfer can
take place. It takes quite a bit of time and effort to get all
the paperwork together. Waiting until everything is ready
to be signed all at the same time makes it much easier for
all the parties involved in the process."

"Oh," said Janae. "It seems really complicated."

Dad said, "That is why I asked Mrs. Howell to help
us. She is a licensed realtor, which means she is thoroughly
knowledgeable and has passed her certification exams.
Her job is to help people on both sides of the property sale
complete the requirements so the closing goes smoothly."

Later, after dinner, Jared asked Dad, "Why did you
look at cars if you wanted to buy a house?"

Dad thought a minute and then answered, "Jared,
managing financial matters is never a simple yes or no
process. Opportunities come up, like finding a house, at
the same time a problem comes up with the van. It is a
matter of deciding if we want to spend money to fix the
van or buy a new one while at the same time realizing we
may have found the home we have wanted for a long time.

"One economic reality is any time you spend your
money for a certain thing, all other possibilities go away."

Jared said, "I don't understand."

Dad said, "Jared, suppose I gave you and Janae each
$100.00. Let's suppose Janae decided to put her money in
her savings account immediately. Let's also suppose that
on our way to the bank, we stopped at the mall. Let's sup-

pose that, while there, you saw a new bike ramp that cost $45 and a DVD you have been wanting that cost $13. Let's suppose you bought them both. You would have spent $63, roughly two thirds of the money you had in your pocket. We proceed to the bank and you deposit $37. Janae deposits all $100.

"We'll also suppose the next day a new bike is advertised. It has a new style drive chain-totally different from your old bike. It costs $100. You would like to buy it and had the money earlier, but because you already spent part of it, your $100 has lost that opportunity. No matter what, a new line of clothes, new bike, whatever new products are offered, you have already used up $63 worth of opportunity. It is traded, or spent, for other things.

"Janae, on the other hand, has retained all the possibilities. By saving her money, she can invest it and have it earn money for her, increasing her net worth without any more effort at all, or she can get the money out and spend it next week, next month or next year."

"I see," said Jared. "Were you thinking about a house while you were looking at vans?"

"Yes," answered Dad. "We need transportation but we also wanted to stay able to buy a house. That is why I priced the insurance, tag and title costs before I looked at vehicles. One key factor in growing net worth is to find out what the cost of ownership is before you make a purchase. If we had bought the wrong vehicle or even the right vehicle at the wrong time, we may not have able to acquire a mortgage."

"What is a mortgage?" asked Janae.

"A mortgage is a certain type of loan secured by real estate; land, buildings, and leases, things of that nature. It requires legal work to make sure the security or collateral, the property of value pledged against the loan, has a clear title. It is different than a car loan or consumer debt."

"Dad, Mrs. Duke said making loans may not be a good idea for your net worth," Janae said, looking worried.

"Well, Janae, she is right. A consumer must always be aware of how much debt is pledged against his income. There are good reasons to make loans; for example, to buy a car. In some areas it would be impossible to get to work without a car, while in other areas, a car is only a huge expense, requiring garage fees in addition to insurance and other fees. A house is of the same nature. Your mother and I sold our house a few years ago and have rented this one. While it may have been beneficial to rent for a while, we feel the time is right to purchase a home. It is worth the interest we will pay for us to have our own house again."

"How do you know if it is the right time?" asked Jared.

"Well, visiting with my friends who are professionals helps a lot. Mrs. Howell knows about home values and I have visited with Mr. Molder about the insurance premiums in this area. It makes a difference what type of house is bought and whether there is a fire station nearby. I also have visited with Mr. Koehler about interest rates and with Mr. McCalla about all the work that must be done in order to buy a house. And of course, we talked with Mr. Johnston. He explained to us about the tax implications of owning a home."

"Wow," said Jared. "You have visited with almost everyone we've met at Finance Camp."

"Yes, we have," said Mom, "and it is time to head to bed so you can get back to camp in the morning!"

Chapter Nine

"Dad, will we still be going to Intermediate School?" Janae asked as they drove by the bus barn.

"Yes. As a matter of fact, I want to take a look at the new building, just see how it is coming along," answered Dad.

He turned at the next corner and drove past a tall new building.

"Wow," said Jared. "What will that be?"

"That, Jared, will be the Glaze Science Annex. When it is completed there will be seven new science labs, each with its own computers and specialized equipment for different types of science studies."

"Why are they naming it after Mr. Glaze? Did he give them the money?" asked Janae.

"No, it is named for Mr. Glaze because the district appreciates all the hard work he has done for the school during his tenure. The money for school improvements and new buildings comes from bond issues," said Dad as he pulled up to the bank. "Ask Mr. Smith to explain. Tell him I sent you!"

Mrs. Lewis greeted the children and did not seem surprised when Jared asked about Mr. Smith.

"Jared, you have been talking with your dad again, haven't you?"

"Well, we were looking at the construction at the school…" began Janae while Jared said, "We just wanted to know how the school pays for…"

"Say no more," laughed Mrs. Lewis. "Mr. Smith is waiting for us to join him. He figured you two would be asking questions today!"

"Hello, Jared. Good morning, Janae," said Mr. Smith as the twins walked in. "Mrs. Lewis tells me you may have questions about bonds."

"We just wondered about the schools, sir. Our parents are buying a house and explained about mortgages, but who pays for the school buildings and things?" asked Jared.

"Well, now, that is a very good question. Many folks attend schools, drive over bridges and down highways, or attend professional ballgames or other events at stadiums without giving any thought to how the buildings or structures are paid for."

Dustin asked, "What is a bond?"

Mr. Smith said, "I think the best way to answer that question is to explain first how it comes about, what creates a situation, or demand, for a bond. May I come at your question from this different direction?"

"Yes," answered Dustin.

"We will use our school as the example. About two years ago a committee appointed by the school board inspected the schools. The committee discovered the school had fallen behind in the area of science. Modern methods of teaching require labs which are rooms with equipment and computers designed for studying scientific models. Without these labs, our school might be graduating students who had not been taught science well. The consequences were that students might not be accepted into universities. The committee recommended building a science annex. The school board asked about designs from different architects. They are engineers who specialize in designing buildings. The board decided on the one they felt was best. When the school board announced the plans, they invited everyone in the community to come to meetings, look over the plans, go over the costs involved and ask questions. A proposition was put on a ballot in an election, meaning each voter in the city was invited to say yes or no to the bond issue proposal. That proposition would increase property taxes. The higher property taxes would be used to make the payments of interest and later, the money loaned, back to people who agreed to invest their money in the bond. It passed, the bond was issued and the work has begun.

"This particular bond issue, then, is technically an invitation for people or businesses to loan money for a promissory note to the school. It states the school will pay interest on that money at 5% in increments over time. People invest in the bonds, meaning they write a check to their broker, the money is sent to the bond company, accountants use it to pay the construction bills and, over time, the interest and principal is paid back by the school with property tax money, earning interest for the investor."

"Mr. Smith, you talked about bridges and roads. Are all these things paid for with bonds?" asked Tracy.

"Yes, mostly. City, county, state and the Federal governments may pay for improvements regularly with bond issues. It can be a good investment for people and is a

good way to raise money to pay for publicly owned buildings and structures," he answered.

Jared said, "You talked about ballparks. Is that government, too?"

"It can be. The decisions about bond issues for cities that want to build large facilities like stadiums vary from place to place but typically those have been financed by bond issues.

"Be aware, though, that businesses can offer bond issues as well," said Mr. Smith.

"You mean you can loan money to a business?" asked Tori.

"It happens all the time, though you must be very careful when deciding who to loan your money to," said Mr. Smith. "Bonds issues are rated by analysts and each has a special rating. There are even things called junk bonds and that is why there are licensed representatives for investments. You should always discuss any investment opportunities with a licensed representative. As a matter of fact, I have asked Mrs. Bates to come visit with you today. Here she is."

Mr. Smith turned to a woman standing in the doorway and said, "Good morning, Mrs. Bates. We have been talking about bonds and licensed investment representatives."

"Good morning," said Mrs. Bates. "I am a licensed investment representative and would like to visit with you about the difference between bonds, which are promissory notes that pay investors interest, and stock, or equities."

"Hi, Mrs. Bates. My grandmother has talked to me about the stock market a lot," said Tori. "She says it goes up and down, but that she just stays the course and calls you if she has questions."

"That is what all representatives do, Tori. We meet with clients and ask questions regarding the stock market, income and possible dates for retirement. That allows clients to decide if they really want to invest their money. If clients feel uncomfortable about the stock market, there are other products that might be a better fit for their investment goals. Licensed representatives ask these questions in order to help find products their clients are comfortable owning."

"What exactly is a stock?" asked Tracy.

"Well, generally speaking, a stock is a certain portion of the value of a company," answered Mrs. Bates. "The company raises money by offering those shares for sale on the stock market. Investors buy the initial offering, which means the money from that sale goes directly to the company. Then later, based on the performance of the company or other reasons, the investor may decide to sell those shares to other investors."

"That sounds really complicated. Is that what Mr. Plummer meant about Market Fresh Stir-Fry doing well on the stock market?" asked Jared.

"That stock certainly looks good, Jared, but that may be due to popularity. Market Fresh Stir-Fry is fairly new and the shares are really in demand now. It takes a lot of time to research a company to find out what it does, if it does it well and if it does well consistently. A company must have a lot of customers with a lot of orders or demand for the service to generate cash flow and profits. Each company listed on the stock market must, by law, publish this type of information quarterly and annually."

Tori said, "My grandmother doesn't like all the stuff she gets in the mail, but she says she gets it because she owns mutual funds."

"Mutual funds are good investments for people who do not want to have to study the stock market," said Mrs. Bates. "They are started by companies licensed to buy lots of different stocks, bundle them together into funds and sell shares of those funds. Analysts read company reports, watch performance and report their findings to the fund managers. These fund managers decide to purchase or sell shares in those businesses.

"Each fund divides the value of all the stock it owns by the number of the stocks it owns, and at the end of each day the price of the fund shares is set for the next day. Mutual funds allow investors to diversify risk and own many types of stock through owning shares of the mutual fund."

"Well said, Mrs. Bates," said a voice from the hall.

Chapter Ten

"Mr. Opella, I am glad to see you," said Mrs. Bates. "Please come in and meet our Finance Camp attendees."

After introductions, Mrs. Bates said, "Have any of you have heard about retirement accounts?"

"Our mom has a 401(k) and Dad talks about his IRA," said Dustin, and Tracy added, "Sometimes they are not happy with them."

Jared said, "My dad says he and my mom each have a Roth account."

Mrs. Bates nodded and said, "Mr. Opella is a Registered Investment Advisor. I have asked him to come here to talk to our school foundation this evening about their investments, but I'd like to ask him to visit with you about retirement plans."

Mr. Opella said, "Thank you. Over thirty years ago, some big companies had pension plans. During the time an employee worked there, some of the company earnings were held back and invested. These plans were designed, after a person retired, to continue paying the worker a fraction of his wage, commonly called a pension.

"As the cost of business became higher and tax laws changed, pensions were phased out and accountants were able to design a plan that allows the employee to desig-

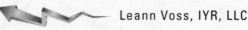

nate a percentage of each paycheck into a new type of investment plan. This plan is called a 401(k). Some companies now offer a matching sum; say 3%, if the employee agrees to set aside 3%. It is like a raise. It is my hope that, if offered, you always accept the terms and enroll in your employer's 401(k) plan.

"Another retirement plan is called an IRA. This plan is something you decide on your own to build, and you may visit with any licensed broker to set it up. You pay into your account each year and determine what stocks, bonds or mutual funds you want to purchase. You must pay attention to the account, just like your 401(k), and talk with your representative about changes you want in your portfolio.

"The last plan we'll discuss today is a Roth IRA plan. The Roth plan is special because, unlike the 401(k) and IRAs, all the money you put into the investment account is always after income taxes are paid. This means the gains from these investments will not be taxed. You must wait until after you are fifty-nine -and-a-half years old to start taking payments, just like the 401(k) and the IRA plans. Workers may have a combination of 401(k), IRA and Roth plans, and these plans form retirement income, in addition to other savings and investments made over time."

"You mean we have to pay into these after we go to work?" asked Tori.

"Well, Tori, let's just say that you do not have to, but if you do not invest for your future, you must save a lot of money to be able to pay for all the living expenses that you will still have after you stop working," answered Mr. Opella. "It is important to learn to pay yourself first, which means writing a check into your savings account and retirement account, before you pay for your home, car, food and other bills.

"When you begin earning wages, it is really important to make saving and investment expenditures first, then decide how much you can spend for a house, car, insurance and food. If you do not decide to do that first and put the money into the accounts, it is possible it will never be done."

"But I thought when I grow up and earn money, I could buy anything I wanted," said Jared, looking glum.

Dustin said, "Yeah, I really want to have a cool car."

"Why get a job if you can't spend the money?" complained Tori.

Mr. Opella answered, "The purpose of earning a wage is to provide income to take care of living expenses. Housing, food, transportation, health care and insurance to protect those things are the basic expenses people are expected to buy as quickly as they finish school and get a job. Sometimes people forget how expensive all these things can be, or just forget to provide things like this. For instance, if you've never paid for health insurance, it would be easy to believe you do not need it. If you've had a car provided for you while finishing school, you may not realize how much auto insurance costs. The same thing can be said for housing. Many people do not realize while renting a home that buying their own home involves the cost of payments, insuring it and the cost of property taxes.

"Without realizing the costs associated with owning these things, contracts for things like cell phones, Internet, cable and other extras may be signed, obligating that income to go to pay those expenses. Others may spend

for consumer goods that depreciate to no value over time. People forget to pay themselves, called savings, and forget to pay into their retirement accounts. They may come to believe they cannot afford to save or pay into a retirement plan. The decision to wait to save and invest is a disastrous one, because you lose time. Time is what all investments need to grow."

"That is my cue!" said Mrs. Lewis. "Thank you, Mr. Opella. Now I would like to introduce Mr. Voss. He is the president of the bank."

"Hello, everyone," said Mr. Voss. "Before I begin, I would like to show you this chart. Janae, would you please pass everyone a copy? Thank you."

"Wow," breathed Jared as he looked at the chart. "I don't understand this."

Mr. Voss chuckled. "You are looking at examples of the magic of compounding. Compound interest can be a really great part of your lifetime savings plan."

Jared was excited. He asked, "What is compound interest? Dad has never mentioned it before!"

Mr. Voss laughed. "That is because I asked him to not mention it to you! I wanted to surprise you, and also to make certain you understood the consequences of spending your money first. Understanding that there are consequences to spending your money, a basic economic equation, is a very important factor in creating savings habits."

"Would you explain that basic economic equation for me?" asked Tracy.

"Yes," answered Mr. Voss. "The basic economic equation simply put is: once money is spent for any good or service, all other options immediately disappear. In other words, you cannot spend money for a hamburger, eat it and spend that money again."

"I understand refunds and things like that..." he added, smiling as Jared piped in, "But what about returns and exchanges?"

"Jared, in the long run, most people buy groceries, games, appliances, tickets to concerts, baseball games and all other purchases and consume them, right? Sure, there are exceptions, but the vast majority of the time the money is spent. Mr. Johnston showed you the high cost of depreciation and how it could hurt your net worth. Mrs. Duke explained how interest would make your purchases grow even more expensive as the goods depreciate, lowering your net worth even more. I want to show you how saving money on a regular basis over a long time can turn small amounts of savings into rather large sums."

date	periodic deposit	prin total invested	interest rate	interest earned in period	with quarterly compounding
1/01/10	$50.00	$50.00	4.00%		$50.00
2/01/10	$50.00	$100.00	4.00%	$0.170	$100.00
3/01/10	$50.00	$150.00	4.00%	$0.307	$150.00
4/01/10	$50.00	$200.00	4.00%	$0.510	$200.99
5/01/10	$50.00	$250.00	4.00%	$0.661	$250.99
6/01/10	$50.00	$300.00	4.00%	$0.853	$300.99
7/01/10	$50.00	$350.00	4.00%	$0.990	$353.49

"For our examples, we have used the number of years you may expect to work after finishing school-about fifty years," explained Mr. Voss. "The magic of this lifelong habit is you have your money work for you as you continue to earn more. Saving money is two-fold; number one, your net worth grows as interest is paid to your account and number two, your money is invested in local communities by banks, helping business grow and develop in your area.

That is the nature of true wealth; it is beneficial for both you and your community."

07/01/60	$50.00	$29,750.00	4.00%	$315.550	$96,9
08/01/60	$50.00	$29,800.00	4.00%	$329.489	$97,0
09/01/60	$50.00	$29,850.00	4.00%	$329.659	$97,0
10/01/60	$50.00	$29,900.00	4.00%	$319.189	$98,1
11/01/60	$50.00	$29,950.00	4.00%	$333.322	$98,1
12/01/60	$50.00	$30,000.00	4.00%	$322.734	$98,2

"You see, by writing yourself a fifty dollar check each month into a savings account that averages 4% over the life of the account, you will pay yourself $30,000.00 and the compounded interest will pay you $68,214.94. That calculation is based on an average of 4% over time. The only effort or work you must do is to pay yourself each month.

"By developing the discipline of paying yourself first, you insure that your hard earned dollars can work for you, building into a sizable account. The only effort, and it is a difficult one, is to develop the habit of always paying yourself first."

"Mr. Voss, how does this work? Is it the stock market?" asked Tracy, amazed.

"No, Tracy, investments are buying stocks, bonds, or mutual funds," said Mr. Voss. "This is saving, which is paying money into certificates of deposit or savings accounts at your local bank. The magic comes from never disturbing the growth; never taking it out. That is why the amount set up in your budget must be paid first, always paid and never touched."

Jared was thoughtful. He asked, "How do you get the money to save if you have a house or car?"

"That is the hardest habit to develop, Jared, and it is the most important step to growing a sizable net worth. Pay yourself first. Make sure you have an ACH online transaction set up to move the money to your savings account, just like a mortgage payment or an insurance premium. Make sure you pay yourself first. Decide what you can afford to pay into your retirement accounts and then pay it into your retirement accounts. Remember, if you do not pay it, it will not get done. After that, decide how much you can afford for housing, insurance, car, groceries, emergencies and other items," said Mr. Voss.

"And, Jared, controlling your spending habits is the next decision. Once you begin earning money, you must decide how you will spend it before you actually spend any."

"My dad calls that a budget," said Janae.

"That's right, Janae," said Mr. Voss. "Deciding before you spend a penny how your paycheck will be spent is an extremely important way to make sure your net worth increases each year. Remember, each purchase you make will affect your net worth, whether it is eating out, buying things or any other spending decision."

"Wow!" exclaimed Dustin. "Did you see this? Look on the back!"

"Yes," said Mr. Voss. "Compounding gets more interesting as you decide to devote more of your income to compounding interest. It is magic, but don't touch it!"

Leann Voss, IYR, LLC

date	periodic deposit	prin total invested	interest rate	interest earned in period	with comp
01/01/10	$100.00	$100.00	3.00%		
02/01/10	$100.00	$200.00	3.00%	$0.255	
03/01/10	$100.00	$300.00	3.00%	$0.460	
04/01/10	$100.00	$400.00	3.00%	$0.764	
05/01/10	$100.00	$500.00	3.00%	$0.990	
06/01/10	$100.00	$600.00	3.00%	$1.278	
07/01/10	$100.00	$700.00	3.00%	$1.483	
06/01/60	$100.00	$59,400.00	3.00%	$354.811	$13
07/01/60	$100.00	$59,500.00	3.00%	$343.612	$14
08/01/60	$100.00	$59,600.00	3.00%	$357.975	$14
09/01/60	$100.00	$59,700.00	3.00%	$358.229	$14
10/01/60	$100.00	$59,800.00	3.00%	$346.920	$14
11/01/60	$100.00	$59,900.00	3.00%	$361.448	$14
12/01/60	$100.00	$60,000.00	3.00%	$350.035	$14

"These charts are examples of what your savings can do for you, if you discipline yourself to saving money over a long time. Your interest rate may go up or may come down, but the magic of compounding will keep working for you.

date	periodic deposit	prin total invested	interest rate	interest earned in period	with comp
01/01/10	$250.00	$250.00	5.00%		
02/01/10	$250.00	$500.00	5.00%	$1.062	
03/01/10	$250.00	$750.00	5.00%	$1.918	
04/01/10	$250.00	$1,000.00	5.00%	$3.185	$
05/01/10	$250.00	$1,250.00	5.00%	$4.135	$
06/01/10	$250.00	$1,500.00	5.00%	$5.334	$
07/01/10	$250.00	$1,750.00	5.00%	$6.190	$
06/01/60	$250.00	$148,500.00	5.00%	$2,850.799	$67
07/01/60	$250.00	$148,750.00	5.00%	$2,759.865	$68
08/01/60	$250.00	$149,000.00	5.00%	$2,888.460	$68
09/01/60	$250.00	$149,250.00	5.00%	$2,889.521	$68
10/01/60	$250.00	$149,500.00	5.00%	$2,797.338	$68
11/01/60	$250.00	$149,750.00	5.00%	$2,928.060	$68
12/01/60	$250.00	$150,000.00	5.00%	$2,834.634	$69

"Remember, there is something else to do with your money besides spending it all. Compounding interest is a wealth builder, and a key component to building net worth. The secret to taking advantage of the magic of compounding is to pay yourself first."

Chapter Eleven

Mrs. Lewis met Jared, Janae and Dad at the door.

"Good morning!" sang out Janae.

"Good morning to you. Are you ready to finish up camp today?" asked Mrs. Lewis.

Janae looked worried and Jared said, "I knew it! Dad said there would be no math, but I bet we have a test. Will we be given calculators?"

Dad laughed. "Jared, there will be no test today. Come on!"

When Jared and Janae entered the community room, they were surprised and happy to see many of the speakers from camp there. As they took their seats, Mr. Voss stood up and said, "Welcome. Yesterday we talked about spending for retirement investments and investments in general. We also discussed saving money by way of savings accounts and CDs and about the magic of compounding. These three choices, spending for retirement investments, spending for investments outside retirement plans, and setting aside money into savings accounts or certificates of deposit, are not generally thought of as spending decisions. But they are. They are spending decisions to build net worth. They do trigger that basic economic consequence; the money becomes unavailable for any other purchase.

"The idea of earning money and being free to spend it as you wish is a basic freedom we enjoy. We can choose, within the confines of what we earn, how much we want to spend for housing, cars, etc. We also choose, again based on what we earn, what clothes we want, if we would like a cell phone, games, computers, televisions, you name it, it is for sale. Typically only federal and state taxes are withheld mandatorily.

"What isn't typically taught, what formed the purpose of this camp, is to bring an understanding to you that if you choose to buy consumer goods and services rather than saving and investing, your net worth will not grow. All the money you earn over your lifetime will be spent. If you spend it all as you earn it, you will not build wealth during your lifetime and when you retire you will have nothing to provide retirement income.

"In general, people build wealth by choosing to save, rather than spend, money they have earned. They make careful spending decisions based on what they feel they need, not on items made popular through marketing. Typically these people spend along pre-set budget lines, which means they have already determined what amount they will spend for any given year, month or paycheck.

"Also typical is a pattern of saving money. A pre-set percentage of savings, non-retirement and retirement investing is determined and reviewed regularly throughout the year. Expenses are planned based on income and other variables which occur throughout the year. In other words, they pay attention to their finances.

"That brings us to the heart of the matter. Most people would like to have a big net worth. In order to build net worth, income must be managed. If you do not pay attention to your finances, they are not managed. But first you must have a belief, a firm understanding inside your mind that guides you to want to manage your money in a way that builds net worth, before any of the management methods will work."

"Mr. Voss, how does that happen?" asked Tracy.

"Yes," piped in Janae, "how do you get that belief?"

"Well, Tracy," answered Mr. Voss, "Mr. Stone can show you the math, the websites and the worksheets which make balancing your demand accounts every month easier, but it will never be done correctly and regularly until you choose to do it. And you will choose to do it regularly only if you believe it is absolutely important for you to spend the time and then actually sit down and balance your account. I would compare this to teaching a young child to walk. Once she starts toddling, she doesn't want to stop and as she grows older, she gets better at it!"

Mr. Voss continued, "Mr. Johnston can explain how to increase assets and keep liabilities at a minimum. You must believe and actively participate in asset management and practice the discipline of spending wisely in order to build your net worth. No one else is in charge of what you choose to do.

"Oh, I see!" chimed in Jared. "When a kid learns to talk, he starts asking questions all the time!"

"That's right, Jared. Communication is really important in finance matters. Mr. McCalla can review financial contracts only if you believe it is important enough for you to have him look one over before you sign. Your

opinion, ultimately, is what determines whether you sign any contract. It is important to understand just believing everyone is honest and has your best interests at heart does not mean it is true. If you sign a contract without any help in understanding what it says, it is because you believed it would be okay to agree to the stated terms.

"Mr. Koehler and Mrs. Duke can look over any financial transactions you may consider. Having a loan officer review any credit offer may help find any hidden costs associated with the transaction before you make a decision to buy. It is also important to remember contracts are binding and interest costs a lot of hard earned money. If you agree to go into debt, any kind of debt, you sacrifice all the interest your money could earn for you while agreeing to pay someone else money you will earn in the future. You lose all your future choices at that point.

"It is vital to understand and believe almost all marketing is designed to get you to spend your money. Advertisements are attention seeking media with this basic purpose in mind, to compel you to believe *you need* what is offered for sale and to motivate you *to spend* your hard earned dollars. That is the total equation. Period.

"Bankers like Mrs. Lewis and our loan officers, attorneys and accountants, investment representatives and insurance agents, are all committed to helping you understand how to manage your income well throughout your life, but only you are responsible for what you believe. And what you believe determines your behavior regarding your money.

"Time is the most valuable asset you have. You use up one day each day. Time is related to money. Interest on a loan is based on how much time it takes to repay it. Time

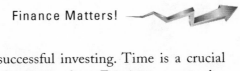

is a key factor in successful investing. Time is a crucial part of the magic of compounding. Earnings spent today lose all potential value time could add to them. It takes a long time to build net worth, and only seconds to spend it. It is what we chose to do over time that determines our net worth.

"We wanted to show you, through this financial camp, some of the ways you may choose to manage your income throughout your whole life. Pay attention to your accounts. Make it a point to meet with your financial professionals periodically. Ask questions about decisions you are contemplating. Make sure you understand the consequences of your financial actions before you sign contracts. Ultimately, your attitude about money management, spending and saving will determine your net worth and how well, or poorly, you will live in the future."

On the way home, Jared said, "Dad, I am thinking about becoming an investment representative when I grow up so I can help people build their net worth."

"That's great," replied Dad.

Jared went on, "Now, Mrs. Bates was telling us about an investment plan for college called a 529 Plan..."

"Jared," said Dad, "Your mother and I set one up for you and Janae not long after you were born."

"Oh. Well, then, I have a question..."